Robert Fulton
A LIFE OF INNOVATION

by Jennifer Boothroyd

Lerner Publications Company • Minneapolis

Photo Acknowledgments

The images in this book are used with the permission of: © North Wind Picture Archives, pp. 4, 16; Courtesy of The Historical Society of Pennsylvania Collection, the Atwater Kent Museum of Philadelphia, p. 6; © National Portrait Galley/SuperStock, p. 8; Picture Collection, The Branch Libraries, The New York Public Library, Astor, Lenox and Tilden Foundations, p. 9; The Granger Collection, New York, p. 10; © Hulton Archive/Getty Images, p. 12; The Mariners' Museum, Newport News, VA, pp. 13, 18, 19, 24, 25; Print Collection, Miriam and Ira D. Wallach Division of Art, Prints and Photographs, The New York Public Library, Astor, Lenox and Tilden Foundations, p. 14; Library of Congress, p. 15 (LC-USZ62-117919); © The Art Archive/Musée de la Marine Paris/Dagli Orti, p. 20; © Brown Brothers, p. 21; PresentationMaps.com, p. 22; Courtesy of: The American Society of Mechanical Engineers and The Mariners' Museum, Newport News, VA, p. 26.
Front cover: © Stock Montage/Hulton Archive/Getty Images

Text copyright © 2007 by Lerner Publications Company

Lerner Publications Company
A division of Lerner Publishing Group
241 First Avenue North
Minneapolis, MN 55401 U.S.A.

Website address: www.lernerbooks.com

Words in **bold type** are explained in a glossary on page 31.

Library of Congress Cataloging-in-Publication Data

Boothroyd, Jennifer, 1972–
    Robert Fulton : a life of innovation / by Jennifer Boothroyd.
      p.   cm. – (Pull ahead books)
    Includes index.
    ISBN-13: 978-0-8225-6458-4 (lib. bdg. : alk. paper)
    ISBN-10: 0-8225-6458-0 (lib. bdg. : alk. paper)
    1. Fulton, Robert, 1765–1815–Juvenile literature. 2. Marine engineers–United States–Biography–Juvenile literature. 3. Inventors–United States–Biography–Juvenile literature. 4. Steamboats–Juvenile literature. I. Title.
VM140.F9B66 2007
623.82'4092–dc22   2006018510

Manufactured in the United States of America
1 2 3 4 5 6 – JR – 12 11 10 09 08 07

Table of Contents

This boat from the early 1800s had to be paddled down the river.

Make It Better

Look at the things around you. Do you see anything that could work better? Could you make a game more fun? Or make a pencil last longer? **Innovation** is making something work better or using it in a new way. Robert Fulton used innovation to make water **transportation** better.

Robert painted pictures on jewelry.

A Talented Artist

Robert was born on November 14, 1765, in Pennsylvania. As a young man, he worked for a jewelry maker. Robert painted very well. His job was to paint tiny pictures on necklaces and rings.

Robert wanted to paint better. He went to Great Britain to study painting with a famous painter.

Robert studied with Benjamin West, a famous painter.

Robert became a good painter. But he was not good enough to earn much money selling his art.

Robert painted this picture of George Washington and Lord Cornwallis.

Robert worked on a new invention.

Using His Talent

Robert thought of another way to use his art skills. He decided to **design** useful things. His ideas would fix problems and make things better. He hoped to sell his ideas. His first idea was to make transportation faster.

Robert drew the plans for many canals.

Robert designed **canals**. Boats on canals could travel faster than wagons on roads. They could deliver **goods** more quickly.

Robert had seen plans for an underwater boat. This gave Robert another idea.

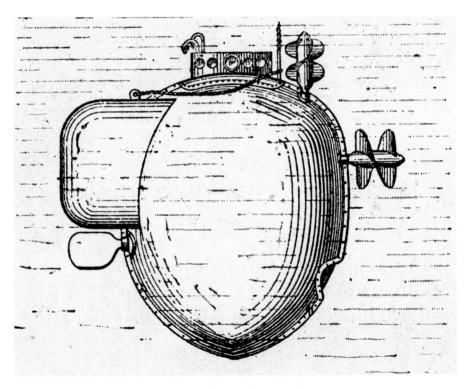

A sketch of an underwater boat.

Robert designed a submarine to sink warships. He took his new idea to France.

Robert worked on his submarine.

Robert met with the leader of France.

Robert talked to the French leaders about his invention. They did not like how it worked.

Robert Livingston was an American businessman.

Robert's Partner

In France, Robert met an American named Robert Livingston. Robert Livingston knew the United States was growing quickly. The country needed a better way to bring people and goods to the new cities. He asked Robert Fulton to design and build a **steamboat**.

Other people had tried to build steamboats. But none of them worked very well.

This early steamboat could only carry four people.

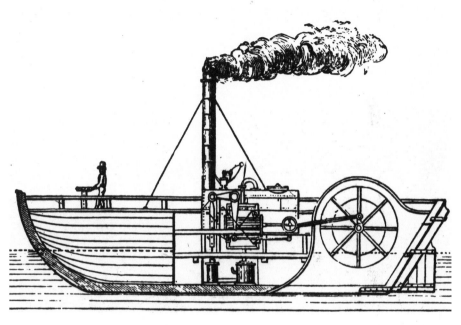

Robert used ideas for other steamboats to make a better boat.

Robert studied old steamboat plans. He used the best ideas to design his boat.

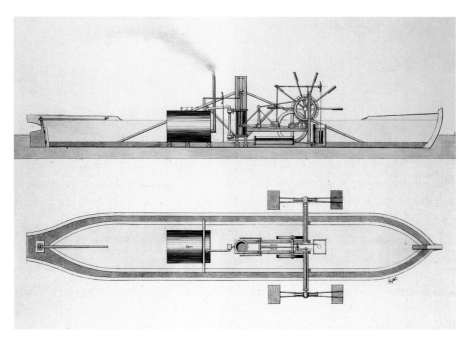

Plans for Robert's first steamboat

He connected two **paddle wheels** to
the engine. The wheels turn and the
paddles push the boat through the
water.

Robert tested his new steamboat. It worked!

People watched Robert's steamboat travel on the river.

NEW YORK
Political Map

⭐ State capital

0   20   40 Miles
|___|___|___|
0   20   40   60   80 Kilometers

N
W · E
S

Glens
Falls

Niagara Falls
Buffalo
Rochester
Seneca Falls
Canandaigua
Syracuse
Saratoga Springs
Cooperstown
Albany ⭐
Watkins Glen
*Finger Lakes
National Forest*
Hudson River
Corning
Kingston
Poughkeepsie
Yonkers
Islip
New York City

22

Success in the United States

The partners moved to the United States. Robert made a steamboat to travel the Hudson River. It would travel from New York City to Albany, New York. This trip usually took four days. To be a success, Robert's ship had to travel faster. He added a more powerful engine to this steamboat.

Robert's boat finished the trip in less than a day and a half. His innovation worked.

Robert's steamboat became very popular. He designed more steamboats to travel on other rivers in the United States.

People read about Robert's steamboat in the newspapers.

26

Innovation

Many of Robert's inventions were not his own ideas. Robert's steamboat was not the first steamboat invented. But through innovation, he improved it. Robert took a good idea and made it better.

ROBERT FULTON TIMELINE

1765
Robert Fulton is born on November 14.

1787
Robert travels to Great Britain.

1782
Robert becomes a silversmith's apprentice.

1800
Robert builds a submarine in France.

1803

Robert runs his first steamboat on the Seine River in France.

1815

Robert dies on February 24.

1807

His American steamboat, the *Clermont*, makes its first trip.

More about Robert Fulton

● Not all of Robert's ideas related to water. He designed a machine to make ropes and another to cut stone. Robert also designed a machine to dig canals.

● Robert painted a panorama in Paris. A panorama is a painting that covers the walls of a round room. Many people came to see this new kind of painting.

● Robert was a member of the group that designed the Erie Canal. This canal linked the Hudson River in New York with Lake Erie. The canal made transportation between eastern and midwestern states easier and faster.

Websites

Robert Fulton
http://www.factmonster.com/ce6/people/A0819870.html

World Almanac for Kids: Robert Fulton
http://www.worldalmanacforkids.com/explore/
inventions/fulton_robert.html

Glossary

canals: a path of water made for boats to travel on

design: to make a plan

goods: things that can be bought and sold

innovation: making something work better or using it in a new way

paddle wheels: wheels with paddles used to make a boat move

steamboat: a boat that uses steam power

transportation: to move things and people from one place to another

Index